Winner of the L. E. Phillabaum Poetry Award for 2011

Southern Messenger Poets
Dave Smith, Series Editor

TALKING ABOUT MOVIES WITH JESUS

poems

DAVID KIRBY

Louisiana State University Press)|(Baton Rouge

Published by Louisiana State University Press
Copyright © 2011 by David Kirby
All rights reserved
Manufactured in the United States of America
First printing

Designer: Michelle A. Neustrom
Typefaces: Whitman, text; Gotham, display
Printer: McNaughton & Gunn, Inc.
Binder: Dekker Bookbinding

Many thanks to the editors of the following journals, in which versions of these poems first appeared: *Boulevard:* "Talking about Jesus with Little Richard," "Wrestling"; *Five Points:* "Big Man's Got the Blues"; *Georgia Review:* "Hey, Gerald"; *Gettysburg Review:* "Paganini's Kickshaw, the Violin Known as 'The Cannon,'" "Skinny-Dipping with Pat Nixon"; *New Madrid Review:* "Ode to Gratitude"; *Pleiades:* "Explaining Gods and Millionaires"; *River Styx:* "The Have-a-Go Pensioner"; *Seattle Review:* "Bo Diddley in Japan"; *Shenandoah:* "The Phantom Empire"; *Solo Café:* "Be Not Inhospitable to Fat Babies"; *Southern Review:* "Bull Cow Moanin' at Midnight," "Talking about Movies with Jesus"; *Subtropics:* "Searching for the Wrong-Eyed Jesus"; *Terminus:* "Old Dog Man"; *Waccamaw:* "These Arms of Mine."

Library of Congress Cataloging-in-Publication Data

Kirby, David, 1944–
   Talking about movies with Jesus : poems / David Kirby.
     p. cm. — (Southern messenger poets)
   ISBN 978-0-8071-3771-0 (cloth : alk. paper) — ISBN 978-0-8071-3772-7 (pbk. : alk. paper)
   I. Title.
   PS3561.I66T36 2011
   811'.54—dc22

                                                      2010024229

this is dedicated to the one I love

Contents

**Talking about Movies
with Jesus**

Talking about Jesus with Little Richard

"I am the beautiful Little Richard," says Little Richard
as he limps to his piano, "and you can see that I am telling
                you the truth" before kicking off with "Good Golly, Miss
Molly" and going into "Blueberry Hill," alternating between
                his own hits and standards by Ray Charles, Hank Williams,
Bob Seger, and such lesser-knowns as fellow Specialty

Records artist Larry Williams ("Bony Moronie") and, withal,
creating "a dream" that is "a memory of the future," as Greil
                Marcus says in *The Shape of Things to Come: Prophecy
and the American Voice*, quoting Steve Erickson's novel
                The Sea Came In at Midnight, though Marcus suggests
replacing "a dream" with "an art." Good idea, Greil!

That's the way art works for me, or at least good art.
So what's bad art? I know, a memory of the past,
                i.e, a memory and nothing more, and you've already had
plenty of those, right, reader? Little Richard only makes it
                to the end of a couple of songs uninterrupted by his own
fizzy glee, biographical bits breaking through ("I was out

there when there wasn't nobody!") as well as musical
preferences ("Kanye West is so beautiful! And I like 50 Cent,
                but I'd rather have a dollah!"), ads for merchandise ("I'll sign
posters after the show, but only the big ones!") and faith
                testimonials ("Don't put a question mark where God
has put a period!"). Also, who else but Little Richard

can say, "I want a big fat white lady to get up on the stage
and dance" and get away with it? "A big fat juicy white lady—
                a juicy one, now! And a big fat juicy black lady, and a big fat
Mexican lady, too"? Before the show, I'd been talking
                to Nancy, a registered nurse who has been to perhaps
a dozen Little Richard shows in the last couple of years

and is wearing a shiny red dress that causes her to "slither,"
she says, as, indeed, she slides out of her seat and nearly
                        onto the floor and gathers herself gamely and plops down
again before starting perhaps her dozenth floorward slide
                    of the evening, though when the Architect of Rock 'n' Roll
issues his summons for beef on the hoof, Nancy, whom

            any gentleman would describe as zaftig, takes off like a shot,
and within seconds she's joined on stage by another twenty
                    women, most disappointingly slim, though, through
the magic of rock, somehow they all turned plump and juicy
                    as they bopped and shook. Speaking of magic, the group
that opens the show is called Falling Bones, a self-described

            "party band" that wisely plays covers of everyone from
the day *except* Little Richard: Chuck Berry, Elvis, the Stones,
                    Johnny Cash. None of the musicians are spring chickens,
but the front man repeatedly and, after a while, convincingly
                    points out that the drummer has just celebrated his eighty-third
birthday, so I borrow Nancy's binoculars, and he doesn't look

            a day over seventy-nine to me. The Falling Bones also say
if it hadn't been for Little Richard, there would be
                    no rock 'n' roll. Not true! It just wouldn't be as good.
There's always somebody before anybody: John the Baptist
                    before Jesus, for example, and God the Father before both
of them. I must be about my Father's beeswax, says Jesus,

            and behold, "Jesus had a huge impact on Christianity,"
as the student wrote in his freshman paper. Speaking
                    of magic again, what is in the black bag that a band member
sets down beside Little Richard's piano stool? Nancy has
                    noticed it during previous shows and guesses that it might
be emergency medical supplies, which is reasonable, being

            as how Little Richard has limped out on crutches, though
it turns out that the trouble is with his hip ("the pain never

leaves!"), so that, in his flowing tresses and spangled blue suit,
he looks like a sea god who has been clipped by a passing
motorboat. Nor does he lack for acolytes, not to mention
proselytes, apostles, and epigones, for even were there no star

performer, the ten-piece Little Richard band puts on a show
that would have the dead dancing, fat and juicy or not,
and its sound is big on guitars and saxes, so that it is loud
but sweet, like World War III fought with candy howitzers.
"Long Tall Sally," "Slippin' and "Slidin'," "Jenny, Jenny,"
"Keep a Knockin'," "The Girl Can't Help It"—they keep

coming, the hits, so that one might say, as Diderot said
of Leibniz, who is best known for his work in philosophy
but who also contributed to the fields of chemistry,
chronometry, geology, historiography, jurisprudence,
linguistics, optics, physics, poetry, and political theory,
that "when one . . . compares one's own small talents

with those of a Little Richard, one is tempted
to throw away one's books and go die peacefully in the depths
of some dark corner." And setting aside for the moment
that Diderot said this not of Little Richard at all, who,
to my knowledge, has contributed nothing to any of these
fields, but of the aforementioned Leibniz, still, it is true

that each of us owes God a death, as someone else says,
and though we may be beautiful, even "old and beautiful,"
as Little Richard describes himself when he engages yet again
with what is clearly a favorite topic, still, as great Achilles
says, "Fat sheep and oxen you can steal; cooking pots
and golden-maned horses you can buy; but once it has left

the circle of his teeth, the life of a man can be neither replaced,
nor stolen, nor bought." All of us will die, some even "fall
dead," as Little Richard says one of the sax players' mothers
did just last week: "She fell dead!" he cries. "Imagine that,

your own mama fallin' dead!" We all want to die in style,
with flowers on the bed table and a scribe to take down

our last words. But then we fall dead: we're making
a blueberry pie for the people that love us so much
                and that we love so much, and they're in the other room
reading newspapers and watching the game on TV,
                when, bam! There's a crash in the kitchen, and they come
running in, and there you are in a welter of pie filling

                and Pyrex, your glasses knocked sixteen ways from Tuesday
and your cotton house dress over your knees. They're grabbing
                their cell phones now: "It's Big Mama," they're shouting,
"she fell dead!" I figure the band members are my best shot
                at solving the black bag mystery, so as I wait backstage
for Little Richard to sign my poster and they leave

                the dressing room for the bus, I ask first the bass player:
"Hey, what's in the black bag?" "Oh, my!" he replies
                and pats me on the shoulder. The trumpet player says,
"Hundred dollar bills—I hope!" A sax player may come
                closest to the truth when he says, " Aw, that's just his
personal stuff." The security guy warns us not to take

                photos or touch the entertainer, but I do want to talk to him,
at least, and I think of Jesus's words to his disciples
                in Matthew 10:16, "Behold, I send you forth as sheep
in the midst of wolves: be ye therefore wise as serpents,
                and harmless as doves," and so, to be wise yet appear
harmless, I say "Willie Ruth" over and over again to myself,

                Willie Ruth Howard being Little Richard's cousin
and someone I'd interviewed earlier this year, so that when
                I finally get up to the front of the line, instead of saying,
"I'm your biggest fan" or "you was out there when there
                wasn't nobody!" or some similarly off-putting claptrap,
I blurt out, "Willie Ruth loves you!" And Little Richard

looks up wide-eyed and begins to speak, and this time I am
reminded not of Matthew 10:16 but of 1 Kings 19, which says,
                    "And behold, the Lord passed by, and a great and strong
wind rent the mountains, and brake in pieces the rocks
                    before the Lord; but the Lord was not in the wind:
and after the wind an earthquake; but the Lord was not

                    in the earthquake: and after the earthquake a fire;
but the Lord was not in the fire: and after the fire
                    a still small voice," and it is with a still small voice that
Little Richard says, "You know Bill?" which is what
                    she told me he calls her, and I say, "I do know Bill, Little
Richard, and have sat with her in her apartment up in Macon,

                    Georgia, and even spoke with you when you called her
on the phone that day," and Little Richard's face lights up
                    and he says, "And you gave her some money!" and I say,
"I did give her some money, Little Richard, because you
                    made me," and we chat for a while, and then he signs
my poster, but before I go, he reaches out to me, and I stick out

                    my hand, and the security guy steps up, and Little Richard says,
"It's all right! It's okay!" and he takes my hand and pulls me
                    toward him, and just then I look over and see the black bag
on a table. Up close, it looks a lot more ordinary than it had
                    before, as though it really does contain his personal stuff.
But what would the personal stuff of Little Richard be like?

                    Does the black bag contain a wallet, a comb, a toothbrush?
Or amulets and charms, things you'd expect to find
                    in the possession of Dr. Nobilio, the Macon "town prophet"
Little Richard remembers from his youth and who terrified
                    his audiences with something he called the devil's child,
the dried-up body of a baby with claw feet and horns?

                    Son House said Robert Johnson made a deal with the Lord
of Night. Little Richard's too godly to have signed such

a compact, but how else explain songs that changed
music permanently, a singer who has gone on for more than
            fifty years and seems as young as yesterday? Just before
he lets me go, probably forever, Little Richard pulls me

            close, and the last thing he says to me is, "Stay close
to Jesus," and I say, "I will, Little Richard." Then afterwards,
            I think, Aw, jeez! I've just promised Little Richard I'll stay
close to Jesus! I mean, anybody can say they'll stay close
            to Jesus, but how many people have promised that to Little
Richard? Talk about a responsibility. Though when I tell

            my son Ian, he says, "Dad, which is the greater responsibility,
to promise Little Richard that you'll stay close to Jesus
            or promise Jesus that you'll stay close to Little Richard?"
and I think, having done the one, why not do the other?
            Jesus, this is my promise: I will stay close to Little Richard.
Early in the morning, I will see his beauty. Late in the evening,

            I will know his love. When "the time going bad now,"
in the words of Macon meistersinger Otis Redding,
            when the Lord of Night holds out his claw to me,
I shall not take it, and though I see the devil's child itself,
            I shall not be afraid. Should I fall dead, let big fat juicy white
ladies dance around me, and big fat black and Mexican

            ladies, too. And should I die in my bed, let him take me
in his arms and let me say, as Keats said to his friend Severn,
            "Severn—I mean, Little Richard—I—lift me up for I am
dying—I shall die easy—don't be frightened—thank God
            it has come." In the midnight hour, I will know him.
When my life leaves the circle of my teeth, I will know.

St. Augustine, October 20, 2007

Paganini's Kickshaw, the Violin Known as "The Cannon"

My physical therapist always says, "Do you watch sports
                on TV, David?" and I always say, "No,"
        and he always says, "Did you see last night's game?"
and I always say, "No," and he always says,
                "Do you think the Knicks (or the Sox or the Browns)
        have a chance this year?" and I always say,
"Tom, if they can avoid injury" or "if they can just
                move the damned ball" or "if they can keep it together,
        then I think they stand a halfway decent chance,"

and he always says, "But what about Hardaway
                (or Arroyo or Wells)?" and I always say,
        "Tom, it comes down to the coaching, doesn't it?"
and we go on like this for hours as he swings my arm
                back and forth like a metronome,
        and when he's through, my arm feels so good,
and we've said so much, and there was no more sense to what
                we said than there is to music or sports or poetry,
        and therefore no wonder the old Greeks loved all three.

Well, four: they liked wine, too. Greek or not, someone said,
                "Wine is sunlight held together by water."
        Lovely expression, don't you think? Makes wine sound
so fragile, which it is, as are words sometimes,
                and here are three illustrations to support that assertion:
        sometimes I call myself "Mr. Wonderful"
when I bring Barbara her coffee, saying,
                "Here's Mr. Wonderful with your coffee,"
        and sometimes she says, "Thank you, Mr. Wonderful!"

though an hour later we could be blackguarding
                each other with language that would scour the hide
        off an alligator! On a somewhat classier level,
consider that, in 642, when Islamic armies captured
                Alexandria, a Greek scholar asked if he might
        take possession of the famous library, and the caliph said

that if the writings agreed with the Holy Qur'an,
                     they are useless and need not be preserved,
          and if they disagree, they are wicked and must be destroyed,

and that was it for the library. Talk about fragile!
                     A final example, this on the lowest level possible,
          at least in the present poem: we are standing in front
of the Assembly Rooms in Bath, and our guide Tony,
                     who has a slight stutter, is saying, "This is where
you'd come to meet someone if you were a lonely cunt,
a lonely cunt, a lonely country parson who wants to get married."
                     That's it in a nutshell, folks; language is indeed delicate,
          weak, watery, frail. Yet also hardy, shellproof, burly,

unassailable! "With twenty-six soldiers I have conquered
                     the world," said the great Johannes Gutenberg.
          So which is it, reader, candy-assed or perdurable, gossamer
or rock-hard? The song is beautiful, but it ends.
                     The athlete looks like a god to us, yet her knees are shot,
          and she will die before we do. And poetry, which we love
more than anything, baffles us, aggravates, makes us want
                     to pull off our clothes and run out into traffic.
          Virgil's biographer Donatus wrote that the poet

used to dictate his poetry in the morning and spend
                     the afternoon working it over "as a she-bear does
          her cubs: licking it gradually into shape,"
which I got from Harriet Rubin's *Dante in Love,*
                     where Rubin herself states that the real challenge
          for a mythic hero is not to slay the dragon
but to tell the story to those who have never seen a dragon.
                     You hit that one on the head, Harriet!
          We must be as brave before a blank sheet of paper

as we are in the face of a fire-breathing lizard.
                     We must summon great powers to our aid.
          We must speak our minds, even if our voices shake.

Humiliation, sorrow, the contempt of our enemies:
                    this is the food of heroes! The things given us
            to transform, that they may be eternal. We must arm ourselves
like warriors, which is why Nicolò Paganini (1782–1840)
                    gave the greatest name ever to his favorite violin,
            his darling, his kickshaw, calling it—wait,

what do you think he called it? Dainty Lace Doily? No.
                    Spoonful of Pudding Spit Up By A Pouty Baby?
            I don't think so. How about Tattered Antimacassar From
A Run-Down Venetian Palazzo or Leaky Sieve Bailing
                    A Battered Whale Boat or Papyrus Found In A Cave
            By A Goatherd Starting a Fire? No? Self Of Steam?
Dog Bark, Cat Cry, Owl Hoot Fading Into The Dawn, Chimera,
                    Willow-The-Wisp, Flash In The Pan Of The Day's
            Blunderbuss? No, Paganini called his violin The Cannon.

Wrestling

Texas trombone player Jack Teagarden is standing on
          a New Orleans levee, and he hears a horn being played
      somewhere across the water, and at first he can't see
anything, just the vague form of a riverboat gliding
          toward him through the mist, but the sound, growing
      louder as the boat nears the shore, is like nothing
he has ever heard—"it was Louis Armstrong,"
          he says later, "descending from heaven like a god,"
and I say, "Louis Armstrong?" and you say, "Why not?"

because who knows what God looks like? If he exists, that is,
          and here we're going to overlook for a moment the words
      of smart-mouth French novelist Jules Renard, who said,
"I don't know if God exists, but it would be better for
          His reputation if He didn't." Very funny, Jules! Meanwhile,
      third-century church father Tertullian insisted Jesus's body
"did not reach even to human beauty, to say nothing
          of heavenly glory," so why not that of a frog-eyed guy with
picket-fence teeth who just happened to blow the best trumpet

then or ever? Though Tertullian screwed up his chance
          for sainthood when he joined the Montanists, sometimes
      called the Cataphrygians, who spoke in tongues
and believed God was one person rather than three, thus allying
          themselves with, not the mainstream, but
      the modalistic Sabellians. As everybody knows. Though I must say
I rather like the way Montanus, the founder of Montanism,
          defended the whole glossolalia thing when he said, "Behold
the man is like a lyre, and I dart like the plectrum. The man sleeps,

and I am awake." Now that's poetry, folks! Which is much
          better than iconography, not to mention iconolatry. Five
      centuries before Christ, Xenophanes said the Ethiopians
fashion dark-skinned gods and the Thracians gods
          with pale skins and red hair, "and if oxen and horses
      or lions had hands and could paint with their hands

and produce works of art as men do, horses would paint
                    the forms of the gods like horses, and oxen like oxen,"
just as Dutch philosopher Baruch de Spinoza would later say

that "if a triangle could speak, it would say that God
                    is eminently triangular," and just as I, who do not resemble
        Otis Redding in the slightest, wonder that God does not
look like the meistersinger of Macon, handsome
                    and broad-shouldered. In that city once I saw
        the lyrics of "I've Got Dreams to Remember"
in the form of a poem his wife Zelma wrote in a schoolgirl
                    hand and gave to Otis when she was, after all,
in her early twenties and close still to the blush of first

love, of thinking how handsome your sweetheart is, how much
                    you love him, how you'll part
        one day, sure, but that won't be for years,
and then you find out it's one year, the plane falling
                    out of the Wisconsin night, trumpeter Ben Cauley alone
        surviving by unbuckling himself and grabbing the seat cushion
that keeps him afloat and listening to the others screaming
                    in the icy water. Or God might look like Chopin,
whatever Chopin looks like: guy I was talking to says

that when someone sits at the piano and plays Chopin,
                    he sees images of beautiful women by lamplight
        looking out on fields of snow, children asleep on a pile
of coats in a bedroom, quiet husbands starved for love,
                    the dignity of dogs, the pleasure of the forbidden kiss,
        the feeling in one's fingers of silk. Religion's serious stuff,
so don't believe anybody who says otherwise.
                    Church insiders say there are two kinds of cardinals, those
who want to be pope and those who *really* want to be pope!

Sometimes when I can't sleep, I say the Lord's Prayer.
                    Why, though? I always manage to get my daily bread,
        and I don't have any debts, at least right now, and the part
about trespassing just sounds to me like somebody walking

their dog in your yard and not cleaning up after it. I think
it must be the Thy Kingdom Come part, which sounds
like something I could support. In Marlowe's play,
Faust asks, "How comes it then that thou art out of hell?"
and Mephistopheles replies, "Why, this is hell, nor am

I out of it." But what if we art in heaven already?
This winter sunshine, this bowl of soup before me,
those cats playing in the backyard: who's to say this isn't it?
Sometimes I think that God listens to Otis Redding
and Chopin the way we do, and I can't say
which makes me happier, that or the idea that when
it's over, it's over. We're looking around one minute,
and then we're not, though we don't know it,
so it doesn't matter. We're there and then not there,

the way a sheet of newspaper leaps into the air
and twists and disappears down a street at midnight,
the wind making its own music. My brother-in-law is
dating a woman whose children are named Isaiah, Molly,
and Heaven. Where'd "Molly" come from? Into the life
of each woman, no matter how godly, a secular boyfriend
must fall. Even better, among the *Mayflower* passengers
were William and Mary Brewster and their sons Love
and Wrestling. Wish my name were Wrestling—wait, it is.

The Phantom Empire

It never got weird enough for me.
—Hunter S. Thompson

A band of horsemen galloping lickety-split across the range are called
                Thunder Riders by kids who've left the city
        to learn about the Wild West at Gene Autry's
Radio Ranch and who now call themselves Junior Thunder Riders,
        not realizing their idols are really residents of radium-rich Murania,
a city 20,000 feet below ground that has attracted

the attention of wicked research scientists who—pant,
             pant-pant—want all that ore! Omigod! It's only eleven
        o'clock in the morning in Baton Rouge,
and my twelve-year-old self has just pushed his fat-tire Schwinn, more rust
        than red paint by now, the tread gone, the horn
and light no longer working, up and down every hill on the four-mile trek

from my parents' farm to the Hart, the Ogden, the Paramount, movie
             meccas, sultans' palaces where I spend
        all my allowance and most of my Saturday mornings in
the company of musketeers and pirates
        and, mainly, cowboys, though I'm drawn less to the big-sky sagas
and more to the serials that precede them, such as

the twelve-parter called *The Phantom Empire,* which I'm watching now.
             The Muranians keep taking Gene Autry
        underground, and he always escapes,
which is good, but when he returns, the scientists try
        to frame him for murder, which is
not good; worse, he has to be back by two o'clock every afternoon

for his radio program or else the contract will be canceled,
             and he'll lose the ranch,
        and the kids will have to go back to the city and breathe gassy air
and drink poisoned milk and not learn any more

western stuff. The blonde and very bored queen of Murania
doesn't get it: her ancestors built the city 100,000 years ago

after fleeing an ice age, and she's very proud of its moving
        sidewalks, robots, and mini-skirted
        male workers in strange barbed hats, yet when she asks Gene
if he doesn't prefer Murania to Texas, he replies, "Well,
        I think the dampness and dead air of your land is more suited
to rats and moles. . . . My business is singing. I sing about horses

and sunshine and the plains. . . . Well, how can anybody
        sing about those things here?
        Kinda makes you feel good to sing, you know." It sure does,
Gene Autry! Though the greatest cowboy song and possibly
        the greatest song ever is not a ditty about blue skies and tumbleweeds
and the great pals you make on a roundup but Stan Jones's

"Ghost Riders in the Sky," in which an old cowpoke
        goes out on a dark and windy day
        and sees a herd of red-eyed cows plowing the ragged skies
and lashed on by gaunt and gluey-gazed ghosts, one
        of whom says, "Cowboy! Change your ways! Or, like us, forever
chase the devil's herd across these endless skies!"

That song is my wake-up call, my guitar-and-snare-drum
        version of the Sistine Chapel and not the salvation part,
        either, but the damnation in which ugly
and deformed-looking sinners are driven onto the shores of Hell by Charon
        and dragged underground by demons
who bite them like dogs. I can't change my ways; I'm twelve years old,

for crissake, and don't have any ways to change. But if I can't
        save myself, who will save me?
        In *The Phantom Empire*, most of the grown-ups are either
wicked research scientists or drone-like Muranians, and even Gene Autry
        seems to be in a daze half the time,
more interested in getting to his microphone by two o'clock every day

than saving the world from evildoers, which is okay, as it turns out,
                        because actually the Junior Thunder Riders
            do most of the heavy lifting in that department,
rigging enough trip wires, kicking enough rear ends,
                slamming enough doors in faces
and bopping enough noggins of bad guys to guarantee that Gene Autry

can put on his show and you and I can stride the face of the earth today
                        conversing in English instead
            of Muranian. Good old kids: where would we be
without them? On the Radio Ranch, life was half epiphany
                and half cordwood, as Emerson's biographer Robert D.
Richardson Jr. said about the day-to-day of his subject,

and there the apple of fire grew on the tree of syntax,
                        as Octavio Paz said of his own poetry. How weird
            it all was, I'd think just before falling
asleep at night, and I'd tell myself that things always
                worked out at the Radio Ranch, which was good, but then I'd tumble
down the rabbit hole and forget everything I'd been thinking

up to that point, yet not before realizing, if only for an instant
                        before the darkness grabbed me,
            though I'd wake what seemed like only minutes
later—how'd that happen?—to sunshine
                and the quacks and clucks of my parents' ducks and chickens,
that it never was weird enough for me, really, never would be.

Be Not Inhospitable to Fat Babies

A fat baby is sitting listlessly in his stroller
when Barbara walks by him on Via Pietrapiana and makes
her famous baby-pleasing "fish
face" at him, and the kid stirs a little
and gives her a tentative smile, and he isn't fat, really,

though let me say this: I don't know what
the Italian word for "chowderhead" is,
but whatever it is, it's going to be
in the Italian dictionary as long as
this baby's alive, or at least as long as this baby's a baby.

Anyway, we go our way, and the baby and his father
go theirs, though we pass each other again
a couple of blocks later, and this time
the kid goes nuts: when he sees his old
friend Barbara, he not only beams at her but grabs

his little restraint bar with both hands
and begins to rock back and forth in ecstasy
because he's just seen the funny lady again,
the fish-face lady—Jesus bird dog,
he's thinking, if only I had language to tell

the other babies about this, how fun it is to see
the funny lady and how much fun I'm having
sitting here in my stroller on Via Pietrapiana,
which is actually not Via Pietrapiana any more
because it has turned into Borgo La Croce!

Although babies probably don't blaspheme.
Not that he's thinking that at all, of course,
because if he had enough language to think
about having no language, then he'd be a grown-up
like us and a baby no more. Not that grown-ups

are exactly infallible in their running of the world,
or maybe you haven't noticed. In the Congo,
                    Chief Nsala rushes into the clearing where Reverend
John Harris and his wife Alice are documenting abuses
        by Belgian rubber gatherers and places before them

        the hand and foot of his five-year-old daughter Boali,
cut off because the chief's village did not meet its quota.
                    And when Barbara went to the police station in Milan
because one of our students had lost her passport,
        "a German couple was there who'd lost

        their four-year-old daughter," she tells me
later, saying, "there were sounds coming out of that woman
                    like nothing I'd ever heard before."
Caliban hears sounds. Pretty ones, though:
        "sometimes a thousand twangling instruments

        will hum about mine ears, and sometime voices
that, if I then had waked after long sleep,
                    will make me sleep again: and then, in dreaming,
the clouds would open and show riches
        ready to drop upon me, that, when I waked,

        I cried to dream again." Is that what babies hear?
If they can't use words, surely they can't understand
                    them, either. What is heaven? Is there language there?
Do angels talk, or do they just hover and smile a lot?
        What is an angel? In the Bronx, five-year-old Abudubacary

        Magassa dies in a house fire, and his classmates
at P.S. 73 tell the teacher not to let anyone sit
                    in the tiny wooden chair at the corner of a low table
because that's where he sat, and now an angel sits there.
        William Blake said his wife was an angel:

        on the day of his death, Blake worked without ceasing
on his Dante watercolors and finally turned to his wife,

who was weeping by his bedside, and said, "Stay, Kate!
Keep just as you are—I will draw your portrait—for
        you have ever been an angel to me," and when he finished it,

        he laid down his pen, began to sing hymns, and,
at six in the evening, after promising his wife
            he would be with her always, died "in a most
glorious manner," as his friend George Richmond
        wrote, saying "he was going to that Country

        he had all his life wished to see. . . . Just before
he died His Countenance became fair, His eyes
            Brighten'd and he burst out Singing of the things
he saw in Heaven," including Jesus—his Jesus,
        that is, the giver of visions, not laws, the union

        of all things human and divine. Blake's Jesus
is a baby, too, but with language. Or maybe
            the language of babies
is laughter. Maybe the fat baby who is laughing at Barbara
        is Jesus—laughing with her, I mean.

Old Dog Man

I'm going to give names to the tall Asian man who's in the garden
          every day with his two old dogs, a beagle and a short-hair mix,
    as I have already to Parrothead, who wears the loud shirt
and louder pants of the Jimmy Buffet fan; Never-Say-Never,
        who jogs faithfully even though she isn't losing
    weight and, truth to tell, seems to be getting bigger; and Where's-

My-Trousers, who does his running in red plaid boxer shorts,
        black knee socks, and polished leather shoes. So I think
    I will call the beagle Yvette because she is pretty
and French and the short-hair Randall because he looks
        American and as though he could take care of business
    if he had to, just as I will call their owner Old Dog Man,

as that name sounds faintly Asian and because he owns
        two old dogs. And if they could speak, they would call him
    Old Dog, since the French shorten everything, turning
"restaurant" into "resto," for example, and "manifestation,"
        or political demonstration, into "manif." One day I see
    Yvette and Randall and Old Dog Man walking into

the Empire Céleste, which is a Chinese resto in my
        neighborhood, and they look tired, as though they are
    returning from a manif for The Declaration of the Rights
of Dog. I wonder what they are going to order and if
        Yvette and Randall can hold chopsticks as well
    as those excellent Chinese soup spoons that allow you to shovel

a lot more broth into your cakehole than our mingy
        Western affairs. If they can do that, then surely they can
    play poker like the dogs in Cassius Marcellus "Cash"
Coolidge's 1910 masterpiece *Looks Like Four of a Kind*
        and others in the Dogs Playing Poker series, though Coolidge
    also invented what's known as the comic foreground,

which is that cardboard cutout that allows you to put
                your face through the oval and appear next to the figure
        of a lifeguard or bathing beauty or, closer to our day, that
of a smiling Richard Nixon or Marilyn Monroe, as though
                you are their best friend. And on another day I follow
        Randall and Yvette and Old Dog Man to the street

where they live, and it is a cul de sac with lots of old
                houses in it, or at least I'm guessing that the houses
        behind the doors are old because the doors themselves
are weathered yet ornate and clearly date from a day in which
                either people cared less about cost than they do now or beauty
        could be found at a reasonable price. The real name of it

is the Impasse Royer-Collard, but I call it Old Door Street,
                although, since you can't enter any of these buildings
        without either a pass code or key to the interior door
or both, I do not know whether they live on the top floor
                or sixth to them, though it would be the seventh to us.
        For their sakes, I hope so, for height is a virtue

in itself, as they know who climb mountains or build
                treehouses or serve their guests "aerial dinners,"
        as aviation pioneer Alberto Santos-Dumont
did in this same city and at the start of the twentieth century
                so that his friends would know what it was like to be above
        the world as they dined at tables so high that

the servants had to climb ladders to serve them.
                Santos-Dumont is also considered the "inventor"
        of the wristwatch for men: that useful accessory had already
been patented years earlier, but it was generally worn
                by women, as men favored pocket watches, though when
        Santos-Dumont complained to his friend Louis Cartier

of the difficulty of checking his pocket watch during flights,
                Cartier went to work and came up with a watch with
        a leather band that could be worn on the wrist so

the balloonist could keep both hands on the controls
                              as he piloted his flying machine around Paris. Something
                    of an obsessive, Santos-Dumont dedicated himself

to ballooning and professed indifference to the opposite sex:
                              "As soon as I feel any affection, I am eager to leave,"
                    he said, for "the feelings would become so powerful
that I should not dare to submit to them." Actually,
                              he was gay. Good! No wife, no kids: he devoted himself
                    to the perfection of the flying machine, for early balloons

were completely at the mercy of the wind, whereas,
                              by adding a propeller and rudders, one could
                    steer with ease and consult one's handsome new wrist watch
at the same time. Article One of the Declaration
                              of the Rights of Dog says, "Dogs are born and remain free
                    and equal in rights. Social distinctions can be founded

only on the common utility," the first part of which is not
                              exactly true, as Yvette and Randall know
                    that dogs with no masters are free to starve and get run over
in the street. They look to Old Dog Man as though
                              he were a god and are thus free in the paradoxical sense that
                    the faithful are always free, but to love and serve one who

looks like a dog to them, a dog *and* a god, for is he not
                              a god who provides kibbles and wah-wah and belly scratches
                    and says, "Good doggy!" whether they have been good
or not? Yvette and Randall are not like the dyslexic agnostic
                              insomniac who stayed awake nights wondering whether
                    there is a dog, because they believe, as Hogarth explains

in his *Analysis of Beauty* (1753), not in some inexplicable je-ne-sais-quoi
                              but a clearheaded je-sais-quoi based on
                    attentive and fully sentient observation of the world. Santos-Dumont
killed himself because he thought the airplane would allow statesmen
                              to fly to one another's countries and explain
                    themselves, but instead they used his marvelous invention

to bomb the enemy into oblivion, so he knotted together
              two of his smart red neckties and hanged himself
      in 1932 at a seaside resort near São Paulo.
Decades earlier, he had flown his marvelous machine around the Eiffel
              Tower: he not only circled it in Dirigible #6
      but waved at Jules Verne, H. G. Wells, and Gustave Eiffel himself,

who were having lunch in Eiffel's penthouse in anticipation
              of just such an event, just as I would like to crawl up
      the fire escape of the building on Old Door Street
and look in the window and wave at Yvette and Randall
              and Old Dog Man. "Old Dog!" say Yvette and Randall
      in the same breath, "who is that!" and Old Dog Man

puts his cards face down so that Yvette and Randall
              can't peek at them and comes to the window and raises
      it and brings it down on my fingers, and as I fall away
from my perch, hoping I land on a Citroën or Peugeot
              or Renault but not a Deux Chevaux—anything
      but a Deux Chevaux—I think I hear him say, "I don't know.

A cat?" At the moment of Santos-Dumont's burial, thousands
              of pilots around the world tipped
      the wings of their planes in a final gesture of respect,
though I have only myself to bid adieu to as I freeze
              in mid-air—a cop could draw
      a chalk line around me, one shaped like the green man on the

crosswalk indicator, though it'd be six feet off the ground—
              over the roof of a beat-up clunker on Old Door Street
      (yes, it is a Deux Chevaux), and to you as well, reader,
pausing before you turn this page, and to Yvette and Randall
              and Old Dog Man, looking down at me from the seventh
      or is it the sixth floor and asking themselves, What next?

Explaining Gods and Millionaires

Sometimes I wish life had those little subtitle screens
             like the ones at Lincoln Center that you turn on
when you want to know what's happening in some opera by Verdi
             or Puccini and off when it's time for you to daydream
      and just make stuff up. You're in Rome with your wife, say,

and she's in the church of San Luigi dei Francesi, sketching
             Caravaggio's *Vocation of St. Matthew,* in which
the future evangelist, who's still a tax collector at this point
             in his career, taps himself on the chest with one hand
      as if to say, "You talking to me?" while he caresses

his money with the other, and you get bored
             and walk outside, where you see a man who looks
exactly like your colleague Barry Faulk, only older and hairier
             and more Italian-y and therefore not very
      much like your colleague Barry Faulk at all; in a situation

like that, wouldn't it be nice to look down at the subtitle
             on your little hand-held unit and find out who the guy is,
especially since, at that moment, he is accosted by
             two gypsy women and disappears around the corner
      with them, which prompts you to go into smart-guy

surveillance mode and pretend as though you're looking
             at the plinths and pendentives and peristyles and other
architectural what-have-yous in the piazza and then whip
             around the same corner as though you're looking
      for an ice cream or a doughnut or a tripe sandwich

just in time to see the man who's not Barry putting
             his wallet back in his pocket and caressing the hair
of the younger, prettier of the two women,
             and you're wondering, did he pay them or they him,
      and if so, for what? Meanwhile, your wife's been

in that church for an hour, so now that the tripe sandwich
           is becoming less of a ploy and more of a necessity
to one who has not eaten since breakfast, you go back
           and tap her on the shoulder and say, "The priest says
you have to leave now," and she says, "I don't see any priest,"

and you say, "He just ducked into the, uh, architrave,"
           and she says, "You mean the sacristy?" and you say
yeah, whatever. The churches are so beautiful over here,
           each more sugary than the next. Such lovely buildings,
such ugly rules: can't use condoms, can't be gay,

can't be a woman and be a priest or a bishop or anything other
           than a baby machine. But the people need their religion,
do they not? Your scofflaw, scapegrace, Voltaire-kissing atheistic
           ass notwithstanding, several billion Taoists, Buddhists,
Baptists, Catholics, and other -ists and -ics, including Jews

of the Reform, Orthodox, and Lubavitcher persuasions as well
           as adherents to both Hinayana and Mahayana Buddhism,
not to mention wiccans, witches, pagans, and panther worshipers
           all believe in some kind of post mortem that transcends
the life of bills and backaches that most of us lead.

Many artists likewise, else no Dante, no Michelangelo,
           no Fra Angelico, Fra Filippo Lippi, George Herbert,
John Donne. Also, many artists use religion whether
           they believe in it or not, as William Blake does in
"The Chimney Sweeper," where little Tom Dacre cries himself

to sleep because his cruel master has shaved his hair, which
           was as white as lamb's wool, and that night he dreams
that "thousands of sweepers, Dick, Joe, Ned, and Jack, / Were
           all of them lock'd up in coffins of black," and an angel
comes by who has a key, and he opens the coffins

and sets the boys free: "Then down a green plain leaping,
           laughing, they run, / And wash in a river, and shine

in the Sun." Now there's poignancy for you, reader! And religion, too.
> Or maybe not, because the poem doesn't stop there;
> it ends the next day, with Tom and the other sweeps waking:

"and we rose in the dark, / And got with our bags
> and our brushes to work," snookered yet again by God
and his wingéd button man, made to wriggle up chimneys
> that will crack their bones, to trade coal dust now for pie
> in the sky later, presuming Blake's being ironic, which is

another thing those subtitles could help with. The only thing
> I don't like about opera is the intermissions:
if I'm shelling out a couple of hundred bucks, I want to see
> a diva stab a duke in the sweetbreads, not a bunch
> of millionaires lapping up ice cream. Wait a minute, though:

of all the arts, none depends on capital as much as this one.
> Sets, costumes, rehearsal time, musicians, dukes, divas,
whatever they call singers who are divas but aren't women:
> it costs money, lots of it. *Ergo ex post facto ubi sunt,* then,
> as the old Romans had it: no millionaires, no opera.

True, you don't see rich folk wandering around on stage,
> dishing out the simoleons to beggars or bribing wardens
to let overweight tenors out of cardboard jails, but that's like saying
> the world doesn't exist because you can't see God.
> Okay, so you don't believe in God; neither do I,

but that doesn't mean I'm not on the lookout for Him.
> When I was in Bloomington, where the Dalai Lama's
brother lives, I visited the Tibetan Cultural Center,
> which the Dalai Lama himself has visited, most recently
> in 1999 to preside over the Kalachakra, a 12-day religious

celebration to cleanse the world of violence,
> though when I tell my guide it seems to me as though
there's still just a little bit of violence going on out there,

she says, "Oh, the Kalachakra also addresses the war
between the gods as well, which you can't see,"

a statement that, regardless of your beliefs, you cannot hear
without casting a glance toward the heavens.
So lap that ice cream, millionaires: you are the gods of opera.
And you gods: you are the millionaires of heaven!
And of our world, too, even if we don't understand it.

Ode to Gratitude

At Dal Pescatore in Canneto sull'Oglio, just outside Mantova

She's weeping, Nadia, as she steps from the kitchen
                    and says, "Thank you for letting me cook for you"
          and takes Barbara's hands in hers and kisses her

on both cheeks, and Barbara says, "No, no, it is I
                    who thank you!" and kisses her and begins to weep
          herself, and they weep and kiss each other,

these two beautiful women, the one who prepared
                    the meal and the other who just spent four hours
          eating it in my company. Sure, it was a commercial

transaction; I mean, money changed hands—a lot
                    of money—just as it does when you pay for anything
          that means a lot to you and that's the best of its kind,

but you can be grateful for anything. A cup of coffee,
                    say. A stick of gum. Toothpick. Why, the paintings
          by the Old Masters are just boiling with *gratitudine*,

which sounds better in Italian than mere "gratitude,"
                    but what doesn't. Take the copy of *Leda* by
          the Leonardesque School in the Uffizi back in Florence:

Leda's so grateful for her four babies, each of whom
                    has just pecked its way out of an egg and is now
          smiling up at its pretty mommy—as Little Richard

says, "Ruby lips, shapely hips!" You can see
                    what's in it for the swan; if all the other swans
          look like him, you *know* he's grateful. "Some old Nazi's

got the original in his schloss," says Barbara,
                    and the old shitheel's grateful for that, though
          he shouldn't be; he should be ashamed, though often

we are grateful even for our shameful acts, for deeds
                              that bespeak our humanity. I myself am grateful
              for Dosso Dossi's *Witchcraft (Allegory*

of Hercules), that is, for paintings I don't understand,
                              just as I am grateful for the scene in
              the film version of *A Room with a View* in which young Mr. George

Emerson rocks back and forth in the branches of an olive tree
                              and shouts "Truth! Beauty!" until the branches
              break and he falls to the Tuscan earth—

grateful for abstractions! And for olive trees, too,
                              the real ones, as well as the fruit they bear.
              I am grateful to all artists named Jacopo or Giacomo

because they remind me of the Neville Brothers
                              singing "Jockomo fee na nay / Jockomo fee na nay /
              If you don't like what the Big Chief say / You got

to jockomo fee nay nay!" And I am grateful for mistranslations,
                              for the guide I overhear telling
              tourists in the Uffizi that the angel who is saying "Ave

gratia plena" to Mary in Simone Martini's *Annunciation*
                              is saying "Hello, graceful," just as I am grateful
              for the man who was arrested in Florida

last year for standing by the side of the highway
                              with a sign that said "Hi, Hitler!" because that's
              what he thought the Nazis were saying in the movies.

I'm grateful for Giambologna, aka John of Bologna—
                              grateful for lunch meat! Grateful for lunch,
              grateful for the little sandwich I have at I Fratellini

on the Via dei Cimatori or the larger one at Noë
                              in the Volta di San Piero, either one washed down
              with a half glass of rough red wine,

and grateful for Ghirlandaio or The Garland Maker,
>   whose *Cenacolo* in the Convent of San Marco
>   proves definitively what Jesus and his disciples

were eating at the Last Supper: cherries! I'm *very*
>   grateful for cherries! Besides, his name always
>   reminds me of Boots Garland, my high school

football coach, whose real first name was Muriel,
>   which is not much of a name for a football coach,
>   just as I'm sure that Yelberton Abraham "Y. A."

Tittle was not an especially macho name for
>   the former New York Giants quarterback and Pro
>   Football Hall of Famer, but then I'm more grateful

for life's little contradictions than I am for almost
>   anything else for which I give a jot or a tittle
>   or a tittie. And because I had polio when I was a child,

I am grateful to Dr. Lawrence Van Gelder for catching
>   the disease early so that I only had to wear braces
>   for a couple of years and not spend the rest of my days

looking at life through the rearview mirror of an iron lung.
>   I am very grateful not to be Rigoletto: "To be
>   deformed!" he cries. "And a clown!"

And is he rewarded for his sufferings?
>   Do his hump and the contempt men hurl at him
>   make him happier, stronger, wiser? For the answer

to that one, reader, fast-forward to the end
>   of Act Three, where Rigoletto, who has paid
>   the bandit Sparafucile to kill the womanizing duke

and thus spare his daughter Gilda from his depredations,
>   receives a bag with a corpse in it, though when
>   he hears the duke singing, he opens the bag

and finds Gilda, who revives, says she is glad
                              to die for the duke, despite his mistreatment
              of her, and breathes her last. Yet I am grateful

for the music, especially "La Donna è Mobile." Which isn't
                              true! For men are just as fickle
              as women, though I am also grateful for lies, just as I am

grateful for my colleague Luca, who comes into
                              the staff room moaning *O che stanchezza!* after
              his three-hour class—grateful for exhaustion,

for the weariness that sends us into a nap that is like
                              death yet from which we emerge childlike
              in our happiness and ready to be grateful again!

For that matter, I'm grateful for death, which rids the world
                              of tyrants but also saints whom we love more than
              we would if they lived forever and became tiresome

and which will rid the world of us before long,
                              though after that, who knows? I am grateful
              for Barbara L. Hamby, and often when I am

kissing her I think she is so sweet that perhaps
                              her flesh is incorruptible, as are said
              to be the bodies of so many of these saints deposited here and there

in the churches that dress up the Italian countryside.
                              And because I do not flatter myself
              that my own flesh is incorruptible, I am grateful to the Speziali

or pharmacy guild of Renaissance Florence
                              and their descendants, the druggists
              who concoct the pills I take for blood pressure and cholesterol,

as well as my present-day physician, the William
                              Placilla, MD who, in prescribing these medications
              for me, told me not to think of myself as a "sick old man"

but one who was taking measures to make his arteries
                              more supple and elastic and would soon have
              "the circulatory system of a 20-year-old, you'll see."

Surely Antonio Sabatini, restaurateur and the husband
                              of the previously mentioned Nadia, thinks her flesh
              is sweet, whether or not he believes that it is

incorruptible and will be reunited with his
                              in the hereafter. I don't believe in heaven, reader,
              though I wouldn't mind coming back for another meal

at Dal Pescatore, or not even the meal itself so much
                              as the feeling that comes after the meal, the sensation
              of being well-fed but not too and tipsy but not too

and therefore happy but not too or *allegro ma non troppo,*
                              as the composers say, and then seeing Nadia emerge
              from the kitchen and taking Barbara's hand in hers

and saying, "Thank you for letting me cook for you!"
                              and Barbara replying as I look on and ponder implications
              that are not inconsiderable and are suggested to me

by the sight of and will, I'm certain, continue to be
                              suggested by my recollection of the sight of these two
              beautiful women, kissing and thanking each other.

Searching for the Wrong-Eyed Jesus

Alan Walden's got a knife under my nose, the same Alan
          Walden who ran Capricorn Records with his late brother
Phil but is better known for managing Lynyrd Skynyrd,
          and now Alan's sticking this knife in my face and saying,
"You fuckin' ain't here!" and "You didn't fuckin'
        see nothing!" because he's telling me about a night

when he could hear lead singer Ronnie Van Zant
          in a hotel room next to his, and gradually it becomes
clear that Ronnie is roughing up a groupie and, if things
         go unchecked, will kill her. So Alan goes in
just in time to see Ronnie clock the girl, who falls
        and hits a table so hard Alan can hear the bones

in her face break, which is when Ronnie gets up
          into Alan's face and tells him Alan doesn't see fuckin'
anything, he's fuckin' not there, this is none of his fuckin'
         business, and if he doesn't want to fuckin' die himself,
he'd fuckin' better get the fuck out. So to speak.
        Ronnie was "set on ready," Alan says, "and if somebody

was crossing us, all I had to say was 'Get his ass.'"
          Ronnie was always pissed off, as people tend
to be when they come from a world of petty criminals
         and snakehandlers and mamas who can't afford
to get their teeth fixed, people Jesus promised
        he'd minister to, not the rich folk who attend

the megachurches and whose needs Jesus
          spends most of his time tending to these days—
unless, of course, there's more than one Jesus. Let's say
         there's the Jesus who ministers
to the minks-and-Cadillacs set and another for everyone else,
        and let's call him Wrong-Eyed Jesus

after the documentary about Southern
                folklore called *Searching for the Wrong-Eyed*
Jesus and featuring novelist/holy terror Harry Crews,
                      who explains how stories are everything to poor people
and then goes into vomit-making detail about the way
        to cook a possum as well as the even more

important way of burying the parts you don't cook,
              which is to put them in a hole in the yard with the head
positioned so the possum's eyes are looking down,
             because possums burrow, and when that possum
wakes up, he's going to be pissed off that you killed
        him, and he's going to start looking for you, only since

he's facing downward, he's going to dig through the earth
            and get "some little China boy" instead of you, and here
Crews claws at his face and rolls his eyes in agony,
        a dissolute seventy-ish white guy imitating a surprised
Asian kid getting "all bit up" by the possum from hell.
        And all the while that Alan Walden's telling me the story

about Ronnie Van Zant and the groupie, he's rising
            from his seat in the restaurant where we're having lunch
and jabbing a knife in my face and faux-threatening
        me with a look which suggests that first-degree homicide
is very close to being one of the Featured Specials
        on today's menu! You should have heard the cries

of "Check, please!" Alan's story ends with him backing out
          of the room and the rest of the band hovering
nervously in the hall; together, they rush back in and pile on
        Ronnie. The groupie escapes, later taking
a vow of chastity and becoming a novice in the Order of Discalced
        Carmelites—okay, just kidding about that part.

The restaurant Alan and I are eating in is just outside Macon,
        near the trailers and the shacks that are home

to people who are criminals, religious nuts, artists,
             or all three, people to whom a story is just as important
as money or a big meal. These are people who walk the line
         every day, as in the song by Johnny Cash that begins

         "I keep a close watch on this heart of mine."
              What if you don't bury the possum right?
There's a lot of tension in that song, not in
              the words, but in the music, and as everybody knows,
if you have to choose, usually it makes more sense to choose
         the music. Johnny wrote that song about himself

     or, more likely, the self he wanted to be, that is,
             not his chicken-filching mutt of a self but the one
that's like Jesus, even if it's Wrong-eyed Jesus,
             the one who doesn't see so good, who's walking down
a Georgia back road at midnight, and there's a billion
         people on the other side of the earth who've never

     even heard his name, but that's okay, and the devil's
             waiting for him at the crossroad, and when he sees
Wrong-Eyed Jesus has a guitar with him, the devil
             says, "I'll tune that thing for you, if you like,"
and Wrong-Eyed Jesus thinks of all he's done today
         and all he has to do, all the coffee-spilling zombies

     he's got to regulate, guys so lazy they wouldn't work
             in a pie factory, the preacher he's got
to see tomorrow over in Sylacauga who claims there's a Chicago
             warehouse full of third-trimester fetuses,
"some of 'em still alive," and Wrong-Eyed Jesus
         looks away and back and says, "Aw, hell, yeah."

The Have-a-Go Pensioner

"Have-a-Go Pensioner Foils Theft Attempt," it says here
            in the *Irish Times*, having been stopped by a lad with a gun
        who ordered him to turn over his money or have his brains
kicked to the curb, to which the pensioner says, "Kick away,
            my boy, for you shall have fuck-all from me,"
and then "I upped my fist, I did, and gave him one of the best, right

in the face." I want to be the have-a-go sort when I am a pensioner,
            which I won't be for many years, though not so many
        that I can't count them. And think about how I want
to fill them: between now, when I, Dave Kirby,
            a kosmos, of Tallahassee the son, "turbulent, fleshy, sensual,"
blah-blah-blah, am at the height of my powers, riding my bike

ninety miles an hour and publishing poems in the finer magazines,
            also making my wife laugh using a variety
        of time-tested techniques, one of which, at her request,
will not be mentioned here, and the moment when my last
            surviving relative presses the pillow down on my face
and I kick and thrash like a turtle on his back in the middle

of the road, a big black Caddy coming slowly my way, and part
            of me thinking, What the hell, it's no more than I deserve,
        and the other part thinking, How do I want to fill the time
that remains, the seconds or months or years that I'll spend
            upside down and flailing? I'd like to be surprised, I think,
though here I refer only to the good surprises, not the bad

ones, as when you come home after a hard day at work
            and your friends are all waiting for you inside your dark
        house, and when you put the light on, they all jump out
and scream, "Surprise!" and you have a heart attack
            and die. That wouldn't be good. On the other hand,
a cool surprise would be like the one the film maker told

me about when he was planning a documentary on melancholy
and going all the way back to Robert Burton
and all the melancholics of yore but then including
contemporary ones, like Van Morrison, so one night
he and his partners have a meeting at his, the film maker's
house, and Van Morrison is supposed to be there,

and he doesn't show, and he doesn't show, and finally
he shows, just about the time the pubs are closing,
and he's as drunk as a wheelbarrow and not melancholy
enough by half but belligerent instead as well as stupid,
claiming he doesn't know what melancholy is
and has never heard of it and doesn't want to know

and so on and so forth and blah-blah, and the film maker
can't tell whether it's the drink or whether Van Morrison
is really stupid or both, but one thing for sure is that
Van Morrison has to go to the lav, so the film maker
tells him it's down the hall on the right, but Van
Morrison is so drunk or stupid or both that he goes

down the hall on the left, and that's the au pair's room,
and he throws the door open and flings on the light
and begins to shout for the toilet and then realizes
his mistake and crashes out into the hall again
and finds the lav and does his business and crashes
back into the parlor and rants incoherently

at the film maker and his mates for another hour or two
and leaves. Next day, the film maker toddles into
the kitchen, and the au pair is cleaning up after
the breakfast she's made for the kids, and she says,
"You know, I had the strangest dream last night.
There I was in me bed, y'see, and who should come

smashin' into the room and yellin' and throwin' things
about but Van Morrison. . . ." Ha, ha! That'd be
a jolly surprise, right, reader? But most of the time

we sit around expecting the bad kind of surprise, for fear is always
                    with us and in many guises, taking the form of an axe,
say, for Gerald of Wales, who wrote in 1185 that

the Irish "always carry an axe in their hand as if it were
                    a staff. . . . This weapon has not to be unsheathed
          as a sword, or bent as a bow, or poised as a spear.
Without further preparation, beyond being raised
                    a little, it inflicts a mortal blow. . . ." And now here's
the money quote: "From the axe there is always

anxiety. If you think you are free from anxiety,
                    you are not free from an axe." Imagine, anxiety
          even then, all the way back in the twelfth century!
Even a have-a-go pensioner couldn't do much
                    with an angry, axe-wielding Irishman,
though almost certainly he'd have a go at him.

Then again, there are so many forms of having
                    a go, including the decidedly more sissified forms,
          such as having a go at ratiocination. *Par exemple,*
when asked what he had learned from the Jesuits
                    at Clongowes College, James Joyce, whom you'd expect
to say something earthier or more incomprehensible or both,

said, "I have learnt to arrange things in such a way
                    that they become easy to survey and to judge."
          That's a good go, too, even if it's kind of cerebral-y.
But let's say I've had all the goes I'm entitled to,
                    that my last go has gone, and me with it.
Where will my friends be then, and where my darling?

Who will say of me, as Yeats does, "How many
                    loved your moments of glad grace, / And loved
          your beauty with love false or true / . . . And loved
the sorrows of your changing face"? At times I see myself
                    laid out in the rotunda of the state capitol building down
on South Monroe Street, thousands of people shuffling by,

kids saying "Daddy, who's that old dead guy?" and their pas saying,
                    "Shut up, Wendell, he was a famous poet—or something!"
          and at others I see myself being chucked out of life like
a card cheat in a western, tossed through a tavern door
          by a couple of mustachioed desperadoes and told to "get out
and stay out!" Either way, whether I'm given a state funeral

or put out by the curb on a "blue Thursday"
                    so the Solid Waste Management boys can pick me up
          like a crashed-out washer/dryer combo, I want somebody
to say, "Well, he had a go, didn't he?" and somebody else
                    to say, "Um, yes, quite—rather prone to the odd go,
our Dave." And even if they don't, I myself will know

I've had a go and may even be having a go
                    at the last moment, may be upping my fist, not to sock
          some wanker in the puss and get myself in the *Irish Times*
sounding feisty and adorable but to take up my pen
                    and write yet another poem and scrounge around for a stamp
and an envelope so I can send it off to one of the finer magazines!

You poets, aren't you having a go when you take up
                    your pens? You poets remind me of the ninth-century
          Irish monk who wrote "I and Pangur Bán my cat / 'Tis
a like task we are at; / Hunting mice is his delight / Hunting
                    words I sit all night." Great time, night. It's when you bend
"beside the glowing bars," as Yeats says about eleven centuries

later, and remember "how Love fled / And paced upon
                    the mountains overhead / And hid his face among
          a crowd of stars." Wow! Well done, W. B.! Love is
that tall, I guess, is so gigantic that his great ruddy face is thrust all the way
                    up into the fires of heaven. And he's kind of a rube, Love is,
a big-eyed yokel yuck-yucking at the astral wonder on every side

of his hayseed head, his wrists and hairy-knuckled
                    hands hanging down past the clouds, his legs as long

as mainmasts in billowing kneeless trousers that whip
this way and that in the wind and collapse
                        like empty sails and then fill again, his workman's
boots as big as a pair of '51 Cadillacs, as battered and muddy as our hearts.

Big Man's Got the Blues

So the girl in front of the stage hooks her thumbs
        in the top of her dress and pulls it down to show
the boys in the band her sugar dumplings, and Newt
        Collier says, "It's a gimmick," and I say, "Hmm?"
Newt used to play trombone for Sam
and Dave, and he tells me they had a gimmick called "getting
        the Holy Spirit," which means
they'd be working up a sweat and "rocking back and forth

the way church people do" when suddenly Dave
        would fall out and the roadies would rush over
to revive him, and just when it looks as though
        the show will have to be called off
and everybody given their money back, Dave leaps to his feet
and rushes back to his mike—I'm a soul man,
        bah-bah-bah-bah-bah-bah-bah-bah-bah!
And now Newt's saying the girl's plum cakes are a gimmick,

too, that she's with the band, which turns out to be
        the case, because after the show I see her chatting
with them in an amiable rather than a sexed-up
        or groupie-ish manner and then scooting
behind the merch table to hawk their tee shirts, CDs,
and posters, all the while perching on a folding
        chair and making change out of a cigar box
like an enterprising small businesswoman rather than

an ol' skank or sleaze. Newt says Otis Redding told
        manager Phil Walden he *never* wanted to be
on the bill with Sam and Dave again, because Otis couldn't
        dance, and he couldn't stand it when Sam and Dave
would "pull out that goddamned Holy Spirit
gimmick every goddamned show!" Newt says
        that sometimes when they had a soul revue
at the historic Douglass Theatre, where all the great

Macon musicians got their start, a guy would run up
                to the MC and whisper and point to the balcony,
and the MC would shade his eyes with his hand
                and look up there, and a big grin would break out
on his face, and he'd take the microphone and say,
"Ladies and gentlemen, we have a very special
                guest this evening, Mister . . . James . . . Brown!"
And the house would go dark, and there'd be

a drum roll, and a pencil spot would shine down,
                and a guy crouching just under the ledge would
slowly raise a tongue depressor that had a picture
                of James Brown stapled to it. "It was a gimmick,"
Newt says, "but a good one, because it worked."
I met Newt when I was hanging around the historic
                Douglass Theatre and doing background for a book
on rhythm 'n' blues I want to write, and somebody says,

"You got to meet Newt Collier!" so I call with
                the idea of maybe making a date with him some day,
but Newt says, "Where are you now?" and I say,
                "At the historic Douglass," and he says, "I'll be there
in ten minutes," and now we're in the Hummingbird
Soundstage and Tap Room on Cherry Street, and a big man
                comes into the Hummingbird, a really
big man, as a matter of fact, maybe six feet six, 280 pounds,

and Newt, whose first gig was with the Pinetoppers,
                which was Otis Redding's original backing band,
says, "That's what Otis looked like when he walked
                into a room," which makes sense, because, when his father
contracted TB, Otis dropped out of high school
and took up well-digging, which, in the day,
                probably didn't involve a whole lot of power tools.
Anyway, Big Man, which is what we call him

the rest of the evening, looks sad, and when a man
                that size is sad, he's *really* sad, so sad that you have

to work hard at not being sad yourself. Too, Big Man's
        throwing them back like nobody's business, like
he's cruising to get a DWI for not having enough blood
in his alcohol stream. Big Man's going to be toxic—
        if rattlesnakes bite Big Man, they'll die. And I wonder
if he isn't thinking about a girl, and then I remember

Otis's saddest song, which is saying a lot, because
        he had a lot of them—even his happy songs are sad—
though the saddest of them all is "I've Got Dreams
        to Remember," the standard version of which tells
of a man who sees his baby in another man's arms,
and the woman says that other man was just a friend,
        and the singer says yeah, but I saw you kiss him again
and again and again, and every time he says "again,"

it's like a door slamming on your hand, a pipe coming
        down on your head, a nail going into your heart again
and again and again. But there's an even more tortured
        version of the song on the Stax Profiles CD
that Steve Cropper compiled, a version in which the singer says
he dreamed they were walking down the street together,
        him and his girl, and Joe Blow comes up and grabs her,
and she just turns and walks away with him, and you think,

Joe Blow? Not Sam Cooke or Elvis or Muhammad Ali,
        but Joe Blow, i.e., anybody, any mullygrubbing,
chicken-and-biscuit-eating dipstick, only now he's got
        your baby and you're, like, dead, I mean, you can see
what's going on around you and hear people talking
and laughing and having fun, only you're not having any
        of it, you feel the way Muslims feel when they undergo
the "torments of the grave," which is when you die

and are grilled by the angels Munkar and Nakir, and if
        you give the right answers, a window to paradise
opens and you go back to sleep and wait to travel
        to the wonderful place you've just had a glimpse

of, whereas if you answer wrong, demons are unleashed
on you front and back, the grave closes in,
          and your ribs break. Where's my baby? Where
are my friends? Lemme out of here! Maybe Big Man's

been listening to too much Otis and too little
          Little Richard, who, with his pancake
makeup, mascara, and mile-high pomaded 'do,
          is all about good times. Put your hand on your hip!
Let your backbone slip. All y'all beautiful women,
say woo-woo! Now all y'all ol' ugly men, say unh!
          Little Richard is all gimmick—all trickeration,
as fight promoter Don King would say. But so what?

"What if we couldn't always tell a trick from a miracle?"
          Diane Arbus said. Big Man needs a big woman—
not as big as the title character in *The Attack*
          of the 50 Foot Woman, wealthy heiress Nancy Archer
whose encounter with an alien turns her into a giantess
who revenges herself on philandering husband Harry and his mistress,
          Honey Parker, but a good-sized woman nonetheless.
Definitely not the girl who's showing the band

her cupcakes; she'd be too small for Big Man,
          and besides, I don't trust her: it's not that her strategy
isn't working, because all the single men in the bar
          are going nuts, just as the men with dates are waiting
for their wives and girlfriends to look elsewhere
so that they, too, can sneak a peek at her cream
          puffs, cherry tarts, rum babas, sweetbreads,
Christmas puddings. Big Man needs a different kind

of girl: passionate, yeah, but modest in public.
          Though if Big Man's girl attracted any unwanted
attention from your lounge lizard, your dime-store
          lothario, weasel man, major ass-pirate-but-only-
in-his-own-mind boozer-loser-type individual,
there's one guy who could settle his hash. Want to

know who? I'll tell you who—Big Man, that's who!
I wonder who the girl is who put Big Man

in his present predicament. I'd like to sit Big Man
on my knee and let him cry and cry. I'll say,
"Big Man, you're going to find a big woman
one of these days, I mean, not one your size,
but with a heart like yours." And then he'll open
that heart to me. Tell Papa, Big Man. Shoot,
I'll put on a dress and a wig hat, if you want—
tell Mama! And I'll make everything all right.

Bo Diddley in Japan

Bo Diddley, Who Gave Rock His Beat, Dies at 79
—*Japan Times,* June 3, 2008

There's Bo Diddley sitting by himself in a folding chair
       and waiting for the start of the induction ceremony
to the Florida Rock and Roll Hall of Fame, so I say,
           "What songs are you going to play, Mr., um, Diddley?"
and he snarls and says, "Bo Diddley songs," and I think,
       Well, that makes sense, seeing as how, when he appeared

on *The Ed Sullivan Show* in 1955, Bo Diddley
       was asked to sing "Sixteen Tons" but instead sang
"Bo Diddley" and was told by Mr. Sullivan off-camera
         that he'd never work in television again. I try a second time:
"You know, Mr. Diddley, I was one of about
       40 million white boys you liberated from the tyranny

of their parents," and he says "Uh-huh," and then we talk a bit,
       or I talk a bit, and I can tell Bo Diddley's bored because
he's looking around and not paying attention and even starts
         to walk off, so I tell him I've put him in a couple of poems,
and he turns and grabs my shoulder like an osprey grabbing
       a mullet and says, "You ever make any money outta

them damn things?" and I say, "I won't lie to you, Mr. Diddley.
       Except for maybe 50 bucks here or 75 there, I haven't made
a nickel of what anybody would call real money out of
         those poems," and Bo Diddley puts his face right
up into mine and says, "You ever make any real money . . .
       come see me!" I haven't, of course: I mean, the money's

okay as far as what poets make, though nobody would
       mistake it for the dough cleared annually by your neurosurgeon,
say, or wrongful injury lawyer. The main thing is it's gone:
         it disappeared into mortgage payments and college tuition,

and if there was ever any left over, that went toward
      a vacation here or a big dinner there rather than to you,

Mr. Diddley, the big man with the strange-looking guitar
      whose performances were "trancelike ruckuses," as Ben Ratliff
wrote in that *Japan Times* piece, the chunka-chunka-chunk,
      chunk-chunk of your signature beat shaping the songs
of musicians who, let's face it, sold a lot more records
      than you did: Buddy Holly, the Who, Bruce Springsteen, U2.

And now you're dead. And now you live on download,
      vinyl, CD, your listeners cueing up "Bo Diddley's a Gunslinger"
or "You Can't Judge a Book by Its Cover" and then "expiring
      in a spasmodic unharnessing of all the wings of the soul,"
as Nietzsche said any human being would after listening
      to the third act of *Tristan and Isolde,* having put his ear

"to the heart chamber of the world" and hearing
      "the roaring desire for existence" pouring from it,
the "innumerable shouts of pleasure and woe." Diddley-san,
      I prayed for you in every Shinto shrine and Buddhist temple
I passed. I prayed for your spirit to be at peace in death
      since it seemed to be so angry in life, and I prayed as well

for Jerry Lee Lewis, Little Richard, and Chuck Berry, 73 years old
      this year, 76, and 82 respectively, each,
in their way, waking us, as you did, to what George Eliot called
      "the roar which lies on the other side of silence."
They can't last forever. They, too, will say goodbye,
      as did Charlotte Brontë's brother and sisters:

"Branwell—Emily—Anne are gone like dreams," she wrote;
      "one by one I have watched them fall asleep on my arm—
and closed their glazed eyes." In European music, harmonic
      development's everything, says rock critic Robert Palmer;
there's almost no rhythmic variation in Mozart
      as opposed to rock's polyrhythms and rough textures.

Still, who doesn't love Fauré, say, or Górecki?
        At the temple on top of Mt. Koya, I listened for you
in the chanting of the monks, but you weren't there:
                monks don't syncopate. I prayed at the Yasaka Jinja
where entertainers pray, but you weren't there, either.
        And before I prayed for you at the Kiyomizu Temple in Kyoto,

a guard said I should strike a big brass bowl with
        a wooden mallet, so I walloped the hell out of
that damned thing—bang-bang-bang, bang-bang!—
                so loudly that a squad of Japanese schoolchildren
stopped and stared at the crazy gaijin man as he whaled
        the tar out of their sacred bowl, their mouths agape

under their yellow sunhats. And as the sound bounced
        off the columns, I heard your voice in there somewhere;
it disappeared and came again, as though from somebody else's body,
                and it was saying Love to last more than
one day—chunka-chunka-chunk, chunk-chunk—love for real
        not fade away, say love that's love and not fade away.

Hey, Gerald

"Hey, Gerald," I say to Gerald Stern, "are you the pope of poetry?"
and he says, "Yeah—the Jewish pope, not the Nazi one!"
This being at the Dublin Writers Festival, which is a big success,
or at least the audience seems to think so,
and this is even before the free drinks. Earlier I decide
that Gerald Stern is the Dr. Johnson of the Dublin Writers Festival,
making me his Boswell, so at the reception, I say things like,

"Hey, Gerald, I don't get the headlines in the *Irish Times*—
they always say something like 'McDougal Defies
McDermott,'" to which Gerald says, "I'm for McDermott!"
And: "Gerald, is the Ireland we're in the bad Ireland,
or is that the other one?" Answer: "Aw, I like 'em both—
it's the people in 'em I don't get along with!" Before I came
to Dublin, I listened to my Gaelic tape,

and so far I can say "Dean deifir!" which means
"Hurry up!" though I don't know which part is "hurry"
and which "up," as well as "feicim" or "I see,"
a sure-fire conversation prolonger if ever there were
one. While I am talking to Gerald
Stern at the reception, the prettiest little colleen comes up and says
"Muh name's Dympna, and this is muh fairst

poetry readin'!" and I feel like saying, "Yuh, and if it wairn't
for muh wee sharp-eyed wife, you'd be muh fairst Dympna!"
or "If I were young and single and straight—wait,
I *am* straight—I'd be contactin' your great wee sma' Irish da'
to see exactly how many head o' them long-haired moor oxen
he'd be wanting for your fair hand there, Dympna!" And then
I realize that'd be the kind of thing Gerald Stern would say,

not I, so I don't say it. The Temple Bar area, where
Gerald and I are staying, is the Bourbon Street of Dublin,
though without strippers, who are not needed anyway to keep
the hormones flying, thanks to all the "stag" and "hen" parties,

as the cabbie who's taking us around calls them, who roam
the streets in search of interspecies romance, which neither
            finds, bellow and cluck as they may. Every morning

     the friendly hostess in the Temple Bar Hotel breakfast room
            greets me with a cheery "How's your head, sir?" Fine, ma'am,
and if not, it's nothing a full Irish breakfast of egg,
        bacon, sausage, tomato, potato, toast, and both black and white
            puddings won't fix. As I walk around Dublin, I notice
that most Dubliners are either redheads from the Viking influence
            (they don't call him Eric the Brunette, you know)

     or Black Irish thanks to castaways from the Spanish Armada.
            So where are the Celts? If Gerald Stern were here,
I'd say, "Hey, Gerald, where are the Celts?" but since
        he's not, I tell myself they're off somewhere making up more Gaelic.
            I am having trouble getting these people to understand
their own language: why, just a minute ago I gave out
            a cheery "Dia dhuit!" ("God be with you!") to two guys

     and waited in vain for their "Dia is Muire dhuit!"
            ("God and Mary be with you!"). I thought they were bad
scholars or else bad Catholics when they just stared at me, but then one said
        "Ich verstehe nicht": they were just good Germans,
            though not Nazis, I'm so sure. Back at the hotel, I run into
festival organizer and get-it-done gal Ruth Smith and ask her if she thinks
            it's the ladies or the gents who are keeping us awake at night,

     and Ruth says the ladies, "because girls are always cackling
            and giggling and screeching!" and then I see Gerald Stern
and tell him what Ruth said, and Gerald says,
        "Oh, well, it's their country, right? . . . So fuck 'em!"
            The day before, there had been a reception at the Canadian
ambassador's house, and a playwright had asked,
            "Who smokes weed?" and Gerald says, "I do!" so I, who can

     take the stuff or leave it, think, How often am I going
            to get a chance to smoke a joint with Gerald Stern?

So we go to the edge of the ambassador's terrace and assume the stance
        the pot smokers always assume, making a tight circle
            and looking over their shoulder as they pass . . . *something* from
one to another, each inhaling deeply and then pausing bug-eyed
            like a frog trying to free itself from some kid's fist before

        whoooooshing! out a cloud of smoke that doesn't smell like
            anything the R. J. Reynolds company sells,
which is when I remember to talk to Gerald about this item
        I'd seen in the *Irish Times* about the prime minister or Taoiseach
            and his ongoing relationship with a member of his cabinet,
and when I say, "Hey, Gerald, it says here the Taoiseach has been
            carrying on with his Oral Health Minister," Gerald says, "His what?

        "Hunh . . . that's not what we call 'em in Lambertville, New Jersey!"
            As we leave the Canadian ambassador's house, the cabbie
tells us the house across the way is Bono's, and just then the gates swing open,
        so we say, "Stop, cabbie!" so we can see if it's Bono,
            but it's just Bono's leaf blower, who eyes us cautiously; there are
12-year-old Japanese girls out there who would kill for one of Bono's leaves.
            I love Gerald Stern, for he reminds me of things

        I don't even know yet, the way Walt Whitman does;
            in addition to being the Jewish pope, Gerald Stern
may well be the Jewish Walt Whitman. Like Whitman,
        Gerald Stern takes me back to what some call
            "the old, weird America," the peculiar country that existed
before mass media made robots of everybody, a country
            of confidence men, jack-a-dandies, knee-walking drunks,

        and freight-hopping hoboes sneaking through towns slick
            with coal dust, yeah, but also a world of gold rushes
and silver rushes and transatlantic cables and new states
        of the union and high-speed printing presses and all sorts
            of modern tomorrow's-going-to-be-even-better–type stuff!
No wonder Whitman liked everything he saw:
        as Van Wyck Brooks wrote, Whitman liked armies

because he liked looking at soldiers, and armies produce
        soldiers: no armies, no soldiers! He liked an old restaurateur
because he knows how to pick champagne, liked nursemaids
        because they are trim and wholesome, and fashionable ladies
        because they are pretty and gay. Whitman liked money.
He wasn't some proto-hippie, folks. He liked business!
        But he also just loved the bejeezus out of regular folk.

Look what he says in "Song of Occupations," how even
        if "you are greasy or pimpled, or were once drunk, or a thief,
Or that you are diseas'd, or rheumatic, or a prostitute,"
        or let's say "frivolity or impotence" were your problem,
        "or that you are no scholar and never saw your name in print,"
Whitman says, and just when you're about to say, "All right,
        enough already, forget it with the compliments," he asks,

"Do you give in that you are any less immortal?"
        So you are mortal and immortal, in Whitman's scheme:
neither one nor the other but both. Everything works out
        for you: you wife hates you but she loves you, too.
        Your boss just fired you and he just gave you a raise.
Your children are diseased prostitutes and Nobel laureates
        at one and the same time—how'd that happen?

You're a prize fighter, say, and you win and you lose
        every night. And when you step into the ring, the old, weird
bearded guy with the slouch hat who's sitting in the front row
        starts shouting, "O the joy of the strong-brawn'd fighter,
        towering in the arena in perfect condition, conscious of power,
thirsting to meet his opponent." So who's doing all that yelling?
        A hundred and fifty years ago, it would have been Walt

Whitman, but today it'd be Gerald Stern, even though
        he doesn't have a beard. But if he did, I bet it'd be a fine one,
full and bushy like those of the Civil War generals.
        And he does have a slouch hat, one he wore the whole time
        we were in Dublin together and in which he looked very dapper.

Also, I love Gerald Stern because, after we had smoked
　　　　　　　　our joint at the Canadian ambassador's estate and were taking

　　　　　　our cab back to the city, I cackled like one of those
　　　　　　　　hen-party girls outside our window at night
in the Temple Bar section of Dublin when Gerald tells me that he'd read
　　　　in the *Irish Times* that a sports writer once complained
　　　　　　　to Joe Louis that another boxer
"didn't like to take it to the body," and Joe Louis looked at the chump
　　　　　　　　in journalist's clothing incredulously and said, "Who do?"

Skinny-Dipping with Pat Nixon

"That blonde kissed me," says Barbara, and I say, "The minx!"
but don't add that she kissed me, too, then said she and her friend
               are going to pull their clothes off and jump
in the pool and do I want to join them, and I say Yeah, kind of,
               only Barbara's in the next room, just-kissed herself or about to be,

and I'm in enough trouble already: we're at a party following
the National Book Festival, and while nobody told me
               not to speak out against the war in Iraq, it's hard to pretend
nothing is going on as surveillance helicopters whack-whack
               over the poetry tent, and some of the peace marchers have

even plopped down in front of me, so I promise them, if elected,
(1) to bring the troops home, (2) to rebuild the city of New Orleans
               exactly as it was before Hurricane Katrina, and (3) to prevent
or at least minimize helicopter flyovers during all future
               poetry readings, and now my host won't talk to me, and all because

I have put a single raisin of doubt on the government's snowy
white cake of confidence. At the opening ceremony
               the night before, four writers spoke, but they all said
the same thing, which is that, if you work at it and keep smiling,
               everything will be fine. And at the dinner afterwards, I'm talking

to a publishing executive who wants to know how I liked what
the writers said, and I say I about half liked it, and he says
               what does that mean, and I say I like all that Abraham
Jefferson Jackson stuff, all the boilerplate about America the beautiful,
               the sunlit, the fluoride-coated, the vitamin-enriched,

but where's bad America, America the weird, the one that says
"No! in thunder," to use Melville's description of Hawthorne,
               although I suspect it was himself he was talking
about when he said that, and the publisher keeps saying what do
               you mean, I don't get it, and I say doesn't every play or opera

or TV show you like have something dark in it, something
bug-eyed and scary, and he says why would I watch anything like that,
                and I say okay, doesn't every great artist walk
the line between the sublime and the horrible the way Johnny Cash
            heel-to-toes it along the narrow thread between right and wrong,

            between the love of a woman he's known it seems like forever
and some nameless dance-hall pussy, though I don't use
                the "p" word, and the executive says why would
anyone write that way, I don't get it, what are you talking about,
            what do you mean. And then this morning, at the White House

            itself, there were four more speakers, but these weren't even
writers, because if you have too many writers at a book festival,
                people get the wrong idea. So there were two TV
personalities and two basketball players, but they said the same thing
            the writers did the night before: life's good, people are good,

            God loves you. Yet every portrait in the White House
is of a failure: Warren Harding, with his gang of unscrupulous shysters;
                LBJ, who went overnight from world's greatest
president to world's worst; even poor Eleanor Roosevelt, with
            her unfaithful husband and ugly buck teeth. But the portrait

            I come back to again and again is of Pat Nixon, so dignified,
so sad, her hands folded in her lap, her eyes pained,
                her narrow chin almost trembling. You weren't good
enough for me when I was younger, Pat; I thought you scrawny
            and neurotic, and you were married to that evil turd Richard.

            But now I'm the age you are in the portrait, and I can see
how hard it was for you, how different it would have been
                if you'd had a good marriage, a good man.
I would get in that pool with you, Pat. As the guests swirl, unseeing,
            you'd turn your back to me and wriggle out of

            your old-fashioned white undies, then dive in and surface
where I wait and throw your arms around my neck.

I brush your hair out of your eyes and glance down
at your breasts, though I'm too shy to touch them.
     The guests nibble gingered beef and crab-stuffed cherry tomatoes,

     and the host pours another drink, a stiff one this time.
The sky over Washington fills with chrysanthemums, their light dappling
               the water and our pale skin as they flash and boom like bombs
or fireworks, though we can't tell which. Kiss me, Pat:
     heal me, heal the world. You've never been more lovely.

These Arms of Mine

Sometimes interviewers want to know what
dead people I'd like to have dinner with,
                    but my answer to that is nobody.
I mean, I wouldn't mind following Dante around
            and see who he talks to and where he shops and what

his writing schedule is, but can you imagine
trying to have a conversation with Dante?
                    Yeah, he wrote the greatest poem ever,
but his world view would be totally different from mine,
            plus his temper was supposed to have been terrible.

Shakespeare wouldn't say anything, probably;
he'd be storing up bits for his next play. Whitman
                    would probably talk your head off, and then
you'd be bored and not like his work as much as you
            used to. No, I don't want to have dinner with anybody.

But if you're serious about time travel, I'd like
to go to Jamaica in 1967 and be sitting at a table
                    and drinking a Red Stripe in the after-hours club
where Bob Marley is playing, and Otis Redding,
            who is touring the island, comes in "like a god,"

according to eyewitness accounts, and Bob Marley
looks up and begins to sing "These Arms of Mine."
                    Wow. I tell you, I wouldn't be myself.
I'd be Troilus or Tristan or Lancelot,
            crying my eyes out for Cressida or Isolde

or Guinevere. She'd be on the battlements
of a castle in Troy or Wales or England,
                    all beautiful and sad-eyed, and I'd be clanking
up a storm as I drop my lance and brush
            back my visor and pound the table with my mailed fist

while all the rastas look at me and say, "I and I a-go
cool out wit' a spliff, mon!" But my arms
          are burning, burning from wanting you
and wanting, wanting to hold you because
     I need me somebody, somebody to treat me right,

     oh, I need your woman's loving arms to hold me tight.
And I . . . I . . . I need . . . I need your . . . I need
          your tender lips, and if you would let these arms,
if you would let these arms of mine, oh, if you would
     just let them hold you, oh, how grateful I would be.

Bull Cow Moanin' at Midnight

"There's two rivers going through Paris!" says one four-year-old boy
                    to another as the No. 38 bus crosses over from
the Right Bank to the Left, and as they are speaking calmly though
            at the tops of their lungs, as little boys seem required
                    to do, the rest of us can't help but overhear as the other
replies, "No, there's just one river, but it has an island

in the middle!" as he joins his wrists and then moves his hands out
                    and forward to show how the Seine flows
around the Île de la Cité and appears to be two streams, even though
            it is just the one, which stupefies the other little fellow
                    for as long as it takes him to reload his mental cannon
and fire another salvo in an argument that goes on at least until

I have to get off at the Luxembourg stop and in response
                    to which every adult passenger within earshot puts his hand
over his mouth and clamps it shut to keep in the guffaws
            that would make the little guys feel self-conscious and clam up.
                    I don't think they would, though. In my experience,
kids that age don't give a hang for the opinions of grownups;

it's only when we're older that we think, Oh god, I just made
                    an ass of myself, what was I thinking when I said that stupid
thing, and as I think this, I am glad that none of my fellow passengers
            on the No. 38 bus can tell that I, too, thought two rivers
                    flowed through Paris when I first saw them, I mean, it,
though I was twenty-eight at the time. Now at the same moment,

and because the human mind is capable of entertaining
                    simultaneously both perceptions of cuteness and thoughts
of imminent death, some of us who are (not) stifling our laughter
            at the two cute little boys are also nervously eyeing the canvas bag
                    someone has apparently abandoned on the floor
of the bus, surrounded as we are by signs which say we should alert

the driver immediately if we see any unclaimed items, and while
　　　　　　　I am wondering if the bag has been left by the go-to-hell
boys or one of my more forgetful fellow passengers, I notice
　　　　　　that the level of grime and wear on the abandoned bag
　　　　　　　　is approximately equal to that on the shoes and trouser cuffs
of the more or less crazy-looking lady just in front

and to the left of me, though I don't mean my description
　　　　　　　in a bad way, because I've always thought that, if
the go-to-hell boys really want to be effective, they'd do better
　　　　　　not to recruit nervous, perspiring young males dressed like suicide
　　　　　　　　bombers but old crazy-looking French ladies who appear
to have nothing more in their grimy satchels than toiletries

and cat food. Say that bomb does go off, though:
　　　　　　　we'd be flying through the air, the little boys and I, as naked
as babies, and they'd still be arguing like adults, whereas
　　　　　　I'd be laughing like a little fellow. I mean, why shouldn't I?
　　　　　　　　No point in holding back when you're leaving this life
for another: if you can't laugh then, when can you? I've got my bags packed.

Emerson said, "A man wakes up sad every day after thirty."
　　　　　　　I say after fifty, every man wakes with his bags packed!
In Emerson's day, thirty *was* fifty, though it's, like, fifteen
　　　　　　now. But the boys shouldn't die: they should have girlfriends
　　　　　　　　before they do and wives and children of their own
and learn how to drink wine and enjoy it with roast meat

and cheese and discover the joy of hard work
　　　　　　　and of helping others. They should eat between eleven
and twelve thousand French pastries each and dance to fast music
　　　　　　and write their own songs and poems and fly airplanes or
　　　　　　　　at least fly in airplanes. They should travel, as I'm doing now:
when I look down, I see what appear to be 30-foot-long

lizards—it's the megalosaurus with his massive tail and
　　　　　　　three-fingered hands, and the next time I pass over the city,

it's the Parisii of the Celtic Iron Age and then warriors and priests
             and then the whole line of Louies, including the one whose mistress
                      thinks he loves another woman and so commissions
a Black Mass in which her naked body is used as an altar—

that'd be the Marquise de Montespan, over whose splendid form rogue
                      priest Etienne Guiborg invokes Satan as well as Beelzebub,
Asmodeus, and Astaroth while, according to legend, the throats
         of children are cut and their blood drained into chalices
                      and mixed with flour to make the host which he consecrates
over her genitals, sticking pieces into her vagina. "An orgy

followed the ritual," says one account, though I doubt it: I mean,
                      after all that, wouldn't an orgy be, like, an afterthought?
Every time I fly over Paris, it's a new day: the revolutionaries
         kill the king and are killed themselves, Napoleon wins and loses
                      and is sent into exile and escapes and is sent into exile again,
Chopin dies and is buried to the tune of Mozart's "Requiem,"

even though his funeral is delayed for nearly two weeks
                      because the Church of the Madeleine has never permitted
female singers but relents, provided the women remain behind
         a black velvet curtain. Baron Haussmann makes the city beautiful
                      but displaces the poor people when he pulls down their houses.
During the Siege of Paris, Austrian troops ring the city,

and the starving people eat zoo animals: the yak,
                      the zebra, the giraffe, even the elephants Castor and Pollux.
There is a world war, and fifteen million die. At the Folies Bergère,
         Josephine Baker dances wearing only a skirt made of bananas—
                      look, her pet cheetah has escaped into the orchestra pit,
where it terrorizes the musicians! Another war, more dead:

twenty-four million this time. It's the twenty-first century, and
                      Paris smells of Mennon Speed Stick and the diesel exhaust
that pours from the buses, one of which goes up in flames—mine!
         The first time I fly over Barbara, she's crying, but the second time,

she has married again and seems content, if not as happy
as before, though her new husband doesn't seem too bright, and look how

small his dick is! Ha, ha! Still, I'm going to get him: "So many
people, dead and in the grave," said Howlin' Wolf, "Yes,
so many people, dead and in the grave, / I better leave ya now darlin',
'fore I get out my blade," and I think wait, wait, if I just turn
my shoulders a little . . . yes! Now I can go to any year I want:
to 1952, for example, and the Wolf's European tour. Howlin' Wolf

pitched a wang dang doodle all night long, him and guitarists Willie
Johnson and M. T. Murphy, harmonica player Junior Parker,
drummer Willie Steel, and the piano player known only
as Destruction, and as I tuck my arms in and shoot ahead like
a torpedo, I veer to the east and, sure enough, I'm at the first
Ann Arbor Blues Festival in 1969, and there's a train track

just behind the stage, and suddenly the drummer starts playing
"train time" or CHOOGA-chooga CHOOGA-chooga
as Howlin' Wolf starts playing whistle sounds on his mouth harp but also
shouting "A-whoo! A-whoo!" as, in the distance, you
hear an actual train whistle—Howlin' Wolf and his sidemen
have heard the train before the audience does, and they make

it an instrument in their band. The train gets closer and closer, the band
gets louder and louder, and finally the train passes right
behind the stage area, blowing its deafening whistle and
shaking the ground for hundreds of feet around, and as I orbit and do
slow back flips and even hang head down for a turn or two,
the fires of the night sky at my feet softening into the blue-gray

of morning, I see a pair of objects coming over the horizon: it's
the little fellows again, and just before we plunge toward
the charred intersection and the flames collapse and the #38 bus
puts itself back together and continues across the river with us on it,
and they're still arguing, and they don't seem to have noticed
that there was a bomb and that they're dead now, so maybe they aren't—

maybe I'm the one who's wrong. Not Chopin, though. And not Howlin'
       Wolf, also known as Big Foot and, my favorite, Bull Cow:
half male, half female, all godhead in a single ungulate, Latin binomial
       Bos taurus, a hoofed, herbivorous quadruped—"This is for me,"
       said Sam Phillips of Sun Records when
he first heard Howlin' Wolf sing, "this is where the soul of man never dies."

Talking about Movies with Jesus

Luxembourg Gardens, Paris

Those of you who prefer to think about Mary, Queen
of Scots as opposed to all those other decapitated monarchs
should try it here, near this statue,
which always makes me think of Jesus, seeing
as how she was born Catholic and he became one after he'd finished

the Jewish phase of his career. Why "Luxembourg,"
though? Nobody seems to know. Today, the country
itself is the world's only grand duchy, meaning it is ruled
by a grand duke. And who's Jesus
today? Well, let's see: there's Ku Klux Jesus hovering in the sky over

the triumphant Klansmen in D. W. Griffith's *Birth
of a Nation*, but he was probably just having a bad day;
my Jesus doesn't hate people. There's Malibu Jesus,
aka blond and blue-eyed Jeffrey Hunter
in *King of Kings*, whereas a first-century Semite would have looked

like a present-day Palestinian, only smaller, topping out
at around 5'3" and weighing a trim 110 pounds, considering
that he walked everywhere; that'd be Shrimp Jesus,
but no disrespect, because his doctrines
are king-sized. Then there's Buddy Jesus, the one Protestants like.

Protestants say Buddy Jesus walks with them and he talks
with them, but my Jesus wouldn't put up with the off-key
singing and the cheesy lyrics. My Jesus
would be somebody who'd walk right by you
and you wouldn't even notice him; he'd be going to the Titian show

at the Luxembourg museum or stopping to take a snapshot
of the kids sailing boats on the pond or stepping around back
to the orchard to catalog the apples

and pears with names like General LeClerc
and Prince Napoléon and Summer Rambo and Madame Ballet,

and he'd look just like anyone else, only more
Palestinian-y. My Jesus would be a poet, like the Joseph Brodsky who sat
in this same park and looked at this same statue
of Mary, Queen of Scots and wrote twenty sonnets
about her and of whom Professor Alexander Zholkovsky

has written, "Brodsky is a versatile poet, metaliterary almost
to a fault," and "pointedly intertextual" with his "jocular references
to Dante, Schiller, Pushkin, Gogol, Akhmatova, Russian
proverbs and popular songs, Mozart, Manet,
a 1940 Nazi movie about Mary Queen of Scots (*Das Herz einer Koenigin,*

with Zarah Leander), Parisian architecture, and so on."
Now doesn't that sound like what the French call
a *délectable compagnon?* Wouldn't it be fun to take
a stroll through the garden with somebody like that
on a sunny day or even a rainy one or, best of all,

one that's overcast and cool so you could walk along
with your hands behind your back and your overcoat
hanging off your shoulders like Jean-Paul Sartre
and Simone de Beauvoir, though without the infidelity
and bad dental work? I *know* my Jesus would be

pointedly intertextual. And metaliterary, too, though not
to a fault: how can you be too metaliterary? My Jesus
and I would walk all over the place,
past the statues of Baudelaire and Saint-Beuve,
past the ravens, big mothers the size of bulldogs, and stop at the apiary

to admire the bees. "I bet you had a lot of honey
over in Palestine," I'd say, and Jesus would say, "Yeah,
we ate a lot of it over there," and then look into the distance
as though he were thinking about his mom and the apostles
and all the suffering he underwent. We'd walk some more

and stop to get a cotton candy, called *barbe à papa*
or "daddy's beard" in French, and Jesus would mutter,
        "This is not my father's beard." I think Jesus would be
                a little mean to me, but that's okay; God knows we were
plenty mean to him. When we pass a glade with a beautiful

        grassy area where you could have a picnic, I say, "You can
imagine naked people at their ease there, like the lovers
        in *Le Déjeuner sur l'Herbe*," and Jesus says,
                "You're an animal, Dave," and I say, "Of course
I'm an animal, Jesus, just like everybody else. We've all got the reptile

        and early mammal brain, so there's the crocodile
and the horse and then the rest of me. And it's
        David, not Dave. Aren't *you* an animal, Jesus? The Gnostic gospels
                say you kissed Mary Magdalene
on the mouth, and your disciples chided you for it." "I am that I am,"

        says Jesus, and when we get to the tennis courts,
I ask him if he wants to play tennis, and he says,
        "I don't play tennis," though I can't tell whether
                he has played and doesn't like it or never learned
how to play and is embarrassed. Jesus says, "You don't

        take me seriously, Dave," and I say, "I do, Jesus!
I want certainty! I want there to be another side,
        and when it's my time to go there, I want you to walk me over,
                just as we're walking through this garden today."
By now it's early afternoon, and the joggers are gone,

        so we stop for a coffee at the little café just south
of the Medici Fountain and then get up and walk some more
        and come to the bowling green,
                and I suggest a game of bowls, and Jesus steps around
in front of me and stares at me so piercingly that for a moment

        I think he's going to headbutt me, and then he says,
"You ever see that Mary, Queen of Scots movie, Dave?"

And I say, "No, I haven't, Jesus,"
                and Jesus says, "I haven't, either, though I know
that during World War II, Swedish-born actress Zarah Leander became

                the highest-paid star of Nazi cinema, upsetting
Josef Goebbels, who felt that the part should have been played by
                a German actress. But if you're going
                for racial purity, what about a Scottish actress?
Wouldn't that make more sense?" and I say, "It . . . it would, Jesus.

                It really would," and then I shrug and say, "Oh, well,
German-Schmerman, Jesus," and Jesus smiles
                and says, "German-Ethel Merman, Dave.
                Did you know her real name was Ethel Zimmerman?
She was a Jew, like me," and I say, "I don't think there's a whole lot

                of Jews like you, Jesus," and the au pairs who've brought
the little kids to the park for the pony rides and the puppet show
                are rounding them up for the trip home,
                and Jesus takes my arm in his and says,
"And Cary Grant was Archibald Leach." "And Natalie Wood?" I say,

                and Jesus says, "Hold on, that's a tough one, it's—
just a sec . . . Natalia Nikolaevna Zakharenko!" "So,
                Russian?" I say, and the gendarme blows his whistle
                because by now it's sundown and the garden is closing,
"Yeah, Russian," says Jesus, "like Brodsky,"

                and the bigger kids are racing to get their boats back
to the rental stand, and the old duffers who have fallen asleep
                on the benches wake with a start and put their newspapers
                and ice cream wrappers in the trash bins
and start to shuffle toward the gates. "Brodsky's sonnets don't seem to have

                all that much to do with Queen Mary, though," I say,
and Jesus says, "Yeah, they're more about
                his fucked-up love life," and I say, "You say 'fuck'?"

and Jesus says, "I say everything,"
and then he says, "I love the movies," and I say, "But the movies weren't

even invented until the nineteenth century," and Jesus says,
"Look, when was America 'invented'?" and he even makes
the little double hook signs in case I can't
hear the quotation marks in his voice, and I say, "1492?"
and he says, "And what, it didn't exist before then?" and just then the door

of the Luxembourg Palace opens and someone steps out;
it is Edgar Allan Poe, and I say, "Is that Poe, Jesus?"
and Jesus says it is, and I say, "But isn't he dead?"
and he says, "Nobody's dead, David,"
and I say, "Is this . . . is this a movie, Jesus?" and Jesus says, "What isn't?"

Notes and Acknowledgments

"Talking about Jesus with Little Richard"

While researching my book *Little Richard: The Birth of Rock 'n' Roll*, one day I was interviewing the singer's cousin, Willie Ruth Howard, when the Georgia Peach himself called up and convinced me to give her $88. The full story is told in that book.

"Wrestling"

The "guy I was talking to" in this poem is Garrison Keillor. The Chopin images are a paraphrase of a column of his rather than something he said to me directly. But once he and Barbara and I sat in the all-night diner on the Florida State University campus, eating pancakes and talking about poetry until the early morning. So I did talk to him, and later I pillaged his column for images.

"Bull Cow Moanin' at Midnight"

The anecdote about the Ann Arbor Blues Festival as well as the title of this poem are from the Web site of the same name (http://www.novia.net/~cedmunds/).

"Searching for the Wrong-Eyed Jesus"

Searching for the Wrong-Eyed Jesus is a 2003 documentary about marginalized Southerners directed by Andrew Douglas. The title comes from a damaged religious statue made of plaster, and the movie is worth watching alone for the scene in which the narrator sees the statue in a guy's front yard and asks him how much he wants for it, and the guy says, "Five hundred dollars," at which the narrator laughs and says, "I'll give you sixty," and the guy says, "How about sixty-five?"

Some of the images in the final stanza are based on ones in Donald Ray Pollock's prizewinning story collection *Knockemstiff*. And it was Rodney Jones who told me about hearing the preacher claim there's a Chicago warehouse full of live third-trimester fetuses.

"The Have-a-Go Pensioner"

This poem is dedicated to the late George Kimbrell, a have-a-go pensioner if ever there were one.

"These Arms of Mine"

This poem is dedicated to the Redding family, especially Otis Redding's daughter Karla Redding-Andrews and his widow Zelma, for their kindness to me in their hometown of Macon, Georgia.

By my count, Barbara Hamby's name appears in these poems fourteen times, which should suggest the place she occupies in my real life, the one where I dream and write.

She's also my first and best reader, and if you find pleasure in this book, that's due in part to the notes Barbara gave me on individual poems as well as the way she managed the whole manuscript, moving poems around and pulling some out and putting others in their place—picture an air traffic controller wearing a toga and a laurel wreath and you get the idea. Factual errors are all mine, as are the lapses in taste.

Thanks, too, to everyone at Florida State University for giving me work for more than forty years, students and co-workers alike. By now, many of the latter have joined those whom Keats calls "the mighty dead," just as there are people out there too young to know they're going to be my colleagues one day. Jefferson said of the grandson who liked to hang about him, "Like other young persons, he wishes, in the winter nights of old age, to recount to those around him what he has learnt of the Heroic Age preceding his birth, and which of the Argonauts particularly he was in time to have seen." But there are no Argonauts, no fifty-oared ship called the *Argo*, no Golden Fleece. It's just us, folks. Just us.